Gratitude From Attitude to Zoe

Johanna Geiss
Copyright 2015 Johanna Geiss

ISBN-13: 978-0692511732

DEDICATION
Dedicated to the four people I am most grateful for: Jay, Luke, Rebecca, and Helen

Acknowledgments

Thank you Luke Erikson for taking a digital copy of my drawing of the owl and creating four color versions of it and sending it back to me. My posting of your four color versions on my blog is what started the chatter from the group about how fun it would be to color the drawings. You planted the seed.

Thank you Rebecca Erikson for sending me articles on adult coloring books and inspiring me to think this is something I could do. You watered the seed.

Thank you Jay Geiss and Helen Renfro for always believing in me whatever it is I am creating. You were the sunshine that turned the seed into a plant.

Thank you Stacey Lane for taking what started as a gratitude project in my own little world and turning it into a book I can share with the big world. You let the plant bloom.

GRATITUDE
FROM
ATTITUDE
TO
ZOE

A Coloring Book for Children of All Ages

A is for ATTITUDE.

An attitude of gratitude. I ask myself, "Jo, how can you get into an attitude of gratitude? Is it like getting into my clothes? Is it like getting into my car?" Could I maybe get into an attitude of gratitude by lying still for a few minutes every morning when I first wake up and simply feeling grateful that I woke up? Could it be this simple, this easy? Yes! I am still. I immerse myself in the gratitude that I have another day to be alive, to live my life with purpose and meaning. I am instantly in the attitude of gratitude. Then I realize gratitude is not about attitude. It is about practice. I am practicing gratitude. Easy. As the sun comes up, I start practicing other great gratitude goodness.

1. I am in a warm bed with clean sheets in a room with photos of Paris leaves and Venice gondolas.
2. I wake up next to Jay who genuinely loves me for me, imperfections and all.
3. When I do get up I will have a toothbrush and toothpaste and a tongue scraper and 12 hour mouth wash! I am grateful to every innovator involved in that list.
4. There is food in my kitchen. I can eat breakfast.
5. There is clean hot water in my shower, soap, shampoo, and clean towels on the rack.
6. I have purpose in my life.
7. I have a meaningful life.
8. I have at least ten people I love wholeheartedly.
9. I have at least ten people who love me wholeheartedly.
10. I have a son named Luke and a daughter by love named Rebecca who amaze me.

B is for BE PRESENT.

When I picked "be present" gratitude I admit I wondered how it would work out. I am here to tell you it is beauteous! It brought me a freeborn feeling. I am free from all the "look-ahead explorer-type personality" planning what comes next. I am free from all the "what the past brought me that I need to fix" bustle. I could just be here, be now, be in the moment. I am a bee on a flower collecting "in the moment" pollen. I am head over heals besotted with be present.

I soon began to realize I could just take care of right now. I did not have to fix Monday's interview. I could just be myself in the moment today and during the interview on Monday. I did not have to fix my 18 pound weight gain. I could just eat healthy today. I could just exercise today. I have always wondered what the Buddha was teaching. Now I have the beginnings of a clue.

I am grateful. I am grateful for being able to set down the weight of the world and pick up the ounces of the moment. Here I am. Doing what makes me happy right now. I am writing. I am hydrating. I am ready to run on my treadmill. I am creating four scroll ideas in my head for next year's creativity project. I am staying here in my Sunday. How sublime.

C is for CREATIVITY.

My giant-sized gratitude is for creativity. I think of all the creations humans have made. I think of life without human creations. So often we think of what humans have created as a negative. We are the bad ones on the planet, but please stop and consider these perfectly positive productions:

- Music--all of it, all of it, all of it. Can you even *imagine* not having music? Blues, jazz, classical, rock and roll, spiritual, hip-hop, pop and country and blue grass!
- All art work: painting, sculpture, glass blowing, glass fusing and stained glass windows and weavings
- Writings like poetry, plays and fiction and nonfiction and <u>every</u> word on <u>every</u> page. No more books? I cannot even imagine not reading! Without human creativity there would not even be paper to make the pages!
- Movies like *The Quiet Man* and *To Kill a Mocking Bird* and *Star Wars* and *Monty Python* and *Gone With The Wind*, and everything in between, and there is so much of everything in between.
- Fabulous food presented like a gift on a plate.
- Spoken word poetry that I could eat up like a chocolate ice cream sundae.
- Every new thing: cars, trains and airplanes, the rings on my fingers, the flat screen TV on which I am watching--right now--*Arts and the Mind* on PBS; the Crocs on my feet; cellular phones and digital cameras that take amazing videos of baby sea turtles making their first run to the ocean; my wristwatch; incubators and cancer drugs; parades and the circus and cotton candy; the house I live in, the couch I am sitting on...it goes on and on...all of these are created as a result of outrageous overlapping expressions of creativity done by amazing people like you and me.

D is for DANCE.

Dancing gratitude is for babies that bebop and do-bop to the music with the beat before they can even stand and move their feet. Adults can bebop and do-bop too if they allow themselves to be vulnerable in the moment and forget to see who is watching. I smile the biggest smile when I see someone who has made a dance their own. I smile when I see dancing. Dancing is joy out loud. Dancing is the body exploding in joy.

People dance at weddings. Weddings are an amazing embracing of optimism, of the idea that life can be good forever after. Because of that, people dance at weddings. They let the, "We can make it" from the bride and groom wash over their cynical selves and dance gets a chance to come out and play.

When I see two people, who are meeting each other for the first time in a long time, their hugs lead to dancing. They cannot help but rock their bodies and give their toes a bit of a spin. This is especially true at airports where people first emerge at the greeting area, which is one of my favorite places to stand and watch tiny dances of joy.

When I run, I exercise. When I dance, I celebrate life. I do my heart more good when dancing! :)

E is for ENGAGE.

Engage in life. This is my vacation on planet earth. I should not spend it in the hotel room. I engage in day dreaming and playground playing. I engage in imagination often enough to save the world.

I engage in connections. I am hard-wired for connections. I connect with family and friends and my purpose. I engage in activities that move me toward my purpose. I engage in movement. Sitting still is not something I want to engage with...

I engage in writing my narrative about the Creativity Project. I engage in time spent with open-minded creative people at the Denver Art Students league and the Lighthouse Writers Workshop.

I engage in sharing. Keeping my ideas, my time, my money, my talents to myself is small, sharing is BIG.   I engage in sharing how to plant and grow happiness because some people do not know how to garden.

I engage in seeing the spirit in everyone I met today. I engage in saying thank you every time possible. I engage in seeing someone enough to know what to say thank you for. I engage in listening three times as often as I speak. I am grateful for all the ways I engage.

F is for FAILURE.

My first thoughts about failure could easily be about the ever present school days fear of receiving an "F" on an assignment. This grading stigma might be what drives so many of us to avoid any chance of failure. However, I am fascinated by how this fear of failure has transformed into a love of failure as I have aged. Now, I want nothing more than to fail enough times to succeed. I love that being willing to fail is what makes, unquestionably, everything possible.

Vulnerability is the "birthplace of creativity" according to Brené Brown in her TED Talk on *The Power of Vulnerability*. Since my great love is creativity I thought I owed it to my love to meet the family. You have to be willing to fail when you are vulnerable. Embracing failure is akin to embracing creativity's kissing cousin and making this cousin my best friend forever.

Seeing failure as a friend is my key to doors otherwise tightly locked. Failure, it seems, is a fabulous friend. Failure says, "Oh yeah, I am yours anywhere, anytime, anyplace." Only a true friend is that loyal.

Failure is my traveling companion on the road to success. I have to say it is an interesting road, one filled with twists and turns, and ups and downs. The road is surprisingly scenic. On this journey, I am grateful that failure will take me anywhere I want to go, and even bring me back home again.

G is for GREETING.

When I come home from work my cat, Blue, greets me. She is waiting at the door from the garage to the kitchen, cued into my arrival by the sound of the garage door going up. The minute I open that door she starts long winding meeeooooowwwwwssss combined with circles of rubbing around my legs, followed by races to her favorite toy. Perfect greeting.

All of our greetings are this way. They set the tone. They make or break everything coming along behind them. We all get a chance to greet people we know and love, most of us everyday, even multiple times a day. I am grateful when my first greeting from Jay in the morning is expressed by him reaching out and pulling me close for a warm embrace before we start the day. Perfect greeting.

When my Grandmother Currey wrote letters her greeting was always, "Dear Ones." I love that greeting. It fills my heart with joy and my eyes with tears to see it here on my own page. I am grateful to my awesome aunts, Currey women all, who occasionally send me a letter with, Dears Ones, as the greeting because they know I love it. Perfect greeting.

Greeting my son Luke, and my daughter by love Rebecca, has taken on new meaning since they moved from Colorado to Washington. Now we greet on iChat more often than the hugs we use to share as we came through each other's front doors. I am grateful for high speed web + Apple. Perfect greetings! :)

H is for HAPPY.

Ironically, my direct line to happy is gratitude. I did not discover this on my own. I have a spirit guide (woo-woo alert) named Neahma. I met her in a night dream many years ago when I lived in Olympia, WA. When I studied Shamanism she became part of my upper world spirit clan. On such a shaman journey Neahma talked to me about gratitude. She told me to make gratitude lists. If my mind was spinning on a problem I should stop my spinning first by literally, or imaginatively, wrapping my arms around a tree. It works every time. I stop my spin, and I make a list of at least ten things I am grateful for and in minutes I am happy.

The Universe handed me a good shake of the happy brain chemicals. I have known this for years. I am what I call "happy resilient." I bounce back to happy from any other emotion. It is my default state. We all have banner happy days, or even banner happy moments that stand out in our memory book. Here are some of mine. I am grateful to say I know there are many more to come:

- The day I learned to ride a bike all by myself and the day I received a birthday gift of a bike of my own.
- The day my art work was in a junior high art show at the school district.
- The day I found out I was pregnant; the day I gave birth; and every magic day with my son from day one.
- The day Jay displayed how deep his love is for me by crying through our wedding ceremony.
- The day I found out I am here to help people find their lost creative confidence.

I is for INTUITIVE PAINTING.

"I give myself permission to live my authentic life because someday I will be dead." These are the words on the tag attached to my Intuitive Painting Journal. I put them on the tag before I even started my journey into intuitive painting. I was in a journal class on Saturday, June 30, 2012. I had been gearing up to start doing intuitive painting for a full month. I had read Michele Cassou's book, *Creativity Without Limits - Point Zero Painting*. I had set up a painting wall, paper, paint and brushes. I wrote on the first page of my journal, "I have no doubt this represents an intuitive creativity doorway. If I go through it, will I ever want to return?"

My gratitude to intuitive painting is three fold:
1. I can go through the door, spend time immersed in that space and bring back deep secrets when I return. Secrets that change my life.
2. I am inspired to explore the difference between imaginative creativity and intuitive creativity. Both have a place. Both bring gifts to me personally and to my world.
3. Intuitive painting takes me to places in my own self I could not reach any other way. Every time I paint I am closer to becoming me. After fifty-seven years of life I am amazed by how far I am from myself.

On the day I first walked through the door I wrote, "If I just put paintbrush to paper what needs to arrive will. It will take over and do the painting for me as long as my known self stays out of the way. I am in love."

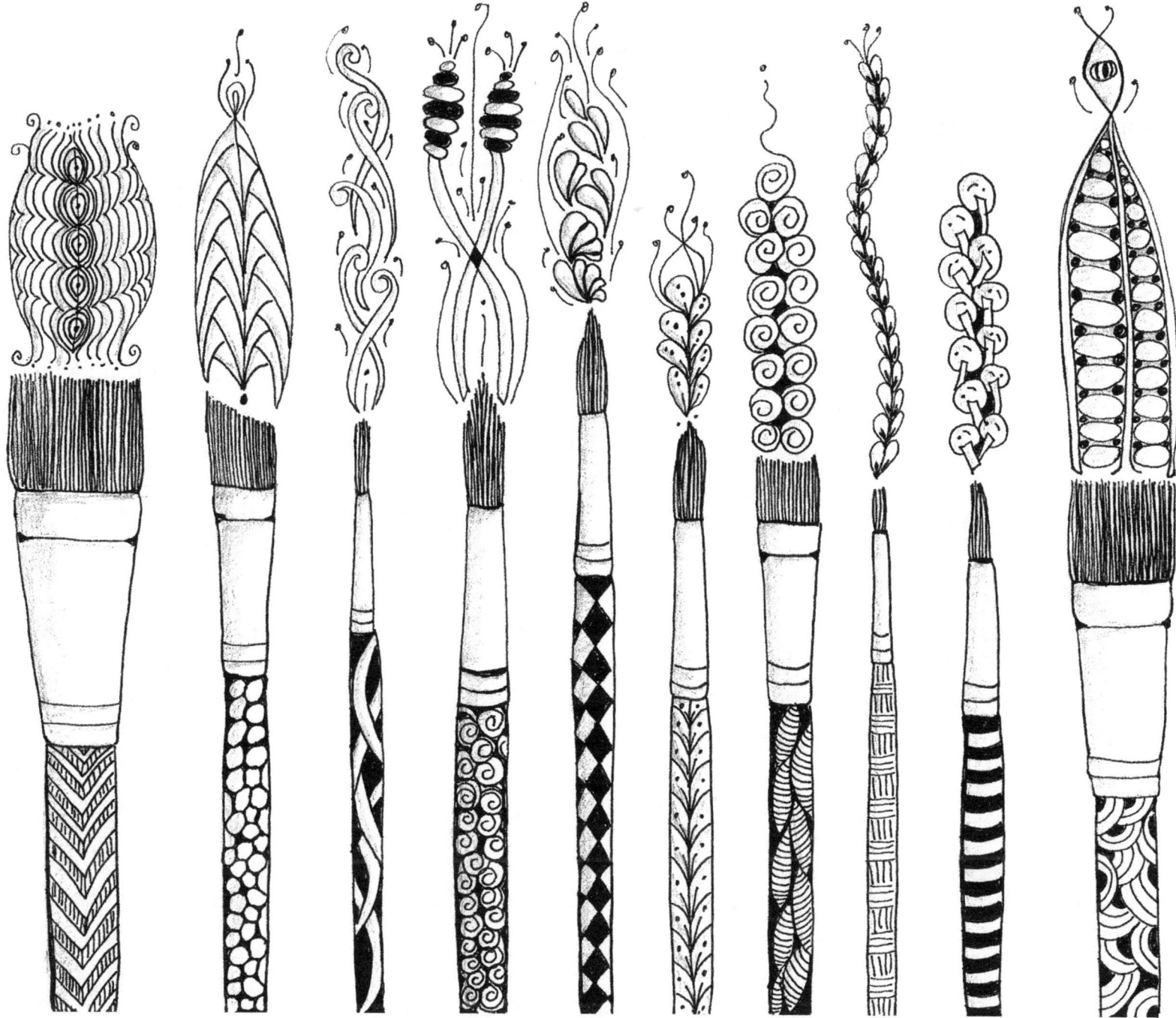

J is for JOURNAL.

My first journal was Luke's baby book. Today I am grateful for those little notes of detail, otherwise long-forgotten over these happy years. I have kept night dream journals and day dream journals, gratitude and travel journals. I took my journal writing up a notch when I read Julia Cameron's book, *The Artist's Way*. Julia introduced me to what she calls Morning Pages, three pages of long hand writing to be done every morning. I always found the most interesting writing happened at the bottom of the third page. My morning pages journals were kept by season--solstice to equinox, equinox to solstice. On each change of season I would burn the previous cycle's pages in a ritual, saying good-bye forever to what I wrote. These days I am keeping journals of my creativity project. This gratitude journal is part of that project. It is a way to combine two of my loves: journaling gratitude and creating art:

- I am grateful to all my gratitude journals and their graceful tracking of the pleasures in my life
- I am grateful for the journals that got me through tough nights of no sleep and abundant worry and fear
- I am grateful for my happiness journal that taught me the delight of saying a daily thank you
- I am grateful for the journal I write in today with its blank pages made from recycled cotton (no trees!) It also supports fair trade
- I am grateful for every inspiring insight I gained as I wrote in a journal--many came to me this way
- I am grateful for the words in my journal, as well as the drawings and photos and found items added
- I am grateful for the journal Jeanette and I shared for a time, handing it back and forth as we had the chance to be in each other's company, reading the words of my friend while she was gone

K is for KISS.

Jay kissed me this morning between gulps of orange juice and immediately said, "Orange juice kiss." There are many types of kisses: movie kisses, friend kisses, kissing on each cheek kisses, mad-passionate-in-lust-with-you-kisses, help the hurt on the skinned knee kisses, dog kisses, old -fashioned on the back of a woman's hand kisses, wedding's you may now kiss the bride kisses, instant messenger emoticon kisses, hello kisses and goodbye kisses. As time goes on I realize my favorite kisses are the ones I get from Jay that feel like *I love even the imperfect parts of you* kisses.

I am most grateful for these kisses in my life:

- Getting to kiss all six pounds and eight ounces of Luke at 11:00 A.M. Central Time, on April 8,1975 when he was 10 hours new.
- Those passionate first kisses with Jay, new love kisses, and the love all of you kisses they became.
- Kissing Rebecca at the wedding to Luke that made her my daughter.
- I love the "Mom" kisses I receive from Liz.
- Kisses from my dear friends like Jeanette, Helen and Nancy. Friends who have been part of my life, these many years of my life. Friends who are sisters.
- I have kissed sentences I have written, and art I have created out of pure love.

Writing *K is for Kiss* makes me wish I shared my kisses with those who matter to me more often.
A kiss is a small gift wrapped in love.

L is for LEARNING.

I recently answered a 240 question survey. The goal of the survey was to identify my top strengths. My number one strength is I am a life-long learner. I knew that without the 240 questions. When I was four years old I talked Penny and Paul into teaching me what they were learning at school during their summer break. I can still remember pointing out to them that was spelled saw when I did it backward. I think that is when they stopped teaching me. I wanted to know things. When Luke was four years old I had to buy a *Why Things Are* book because he wanted to know things. Here is the difference: I wanted to know things; Luke wanted to know why. His physics love affair started early. I am grateful I have learned these things. I am most grateful to know I will learn many more.

- I am grateful I live in a country where girls can attend school.
- I am grateful for my K-12 education.
- I am grateful for my Saint Martin's University education.
- I am grateful for every book I have ever read and I say thank you in advance for every book I will ever read.
- I am amazingly grateful I learned I can be both imperfect and safe. This changed my life.
- I am grateful I learned vulnerability is the birthplace of creativity.
- I am grateful for Ted Talks - Ideas Worth Spreading.
- I am grateful I learned to dance to my own tune.
- I am grateful for all the lessons learned by living life, especially when I dare greatly.

M is for MOON.

I have to admit I have never been able to see a man in the moon. Maybe because my eyesight was so bad as a child, maybe because it makes no sense to me. The moon is a woman.   Mother Moon--that is how I see her, the warm soft light that moves through the night sky and changes her shape from journey to journey. The moon is a woman. Women are the dark, moist, warm side of life. Women synch their blood cycles to the moon when they see it; most of us are inside these days....

When I studied Wicca teachings I learned to embrace and release with the waxing and the waning of the moon. I cast a spell for what I want to grow larger in my life while Mother Moon is also growing from tiny crescent to quarter to half to three quarter to her full round glowing glory. I cast a spell to release what should become smaller or leave my life when Mother Moon is changing from full to three quarter to half to one quarter to crescent to her dramatic disappearance when she becomes new. I become full. I become new.

Clarissa Pinkola Estes tells a marvelous story about people in a village that learn to only be out at night when Mother Moon shines brightly. When she is gone they are to stay in, stay safe and wait for her return. It is a teaching story. It teaches to give ourselves time to be out like our Mother the Moon and time to be in, alone, letting ourselves become new. I am grateful for the cycles of the moon that teach me to honor the cycles in me. I shine at times. I retreat and become new at times. I remember to be new.

N is for NIGHT.

Night is for seeing the stars in the sky, about 6000 on a clear night according to wiki answers. Just think, we forget all about them being there during the day. I am grateful night reminds me there are stars in the sky all the time, just waiting to be seen again.

Night is for comfortable beds, warm blankets and pillows of a certain shape, special to our own heads. I always want to take mine along to sleep on when I travel, but I don't. Night is for arranging my pillows, and when they are "just right" settling in with a book to read for a few precious moments before the words blur and the eyes close.

Night is for sleep that restores our bodies and apparently keeps us sane. Remember the *StarTrek Next Generation* episode when no one slept? We don't want that happening here. I am grateful for night and sleeping sanity. Night is for dreaming where crazy things happen and wild things creep across the boundaries of our rational mind which might be why we stay sane. When you think about that circle you do have to wonder.... I am grateful for night dreams and sanity.

Night is for spooning with Jay who never fails, no matter how deeply he is asleep, to respond to my spoon attack by reaching for my arm to pull me closer. Night is for waking up with Jay and saying. "Look we woke up. We have another day." I am grateful each new day follows a night.

O is for ONE ENERGY FIELD.

There are 400 billion stars in a galaxy. There are 75 trillion cells in a human body. The space in between them all is one energy field. This energy field fascinates me, the same energy field in between them all: my cells, stars in space, your cells, sunshine, rain, my cat, roses, the rain forest, whales and Mars. This is how I now embrace *All is One*. I have struggled for years with the *All is One* idea. I say hello to you across the energy field. Did you feel it vibrating?

Do we feel it vibrating? We should. It does. That is what it does; it vibrates. The idea of our personal emotional vibration having an impact on the one energy field vibration makes sense to me. If there are two violins in a room and you pluck a string on one the corresponding string on the other will vibrate. Resonance: The reinforcement or prolongation of sound by reflection from a surface or by the synchronous vibration of a neighboring object. We are all neighboring objects. Our emotions have a vibration. Stand next to an angry person. You can feel it. Sit with someone who has suffered the loss of a love one. You can feel it. Embrace someone newly and madly in love. You can feel it. I am grateful for the feeling. I cannot imagine life without it.

Here is the thing, I believe there is a collective pool of our vibration. We lift up and go down like an ocean wave in the collective pool. My deepest hope is those of us who are aware lift the vibration of the ones who are not. I am grateful for aware people contributing *good good good -- good vibrations*.

P is for PERSPECTIVE.

Pink sings a song, "Get the Party Started." I think about perspective that way. It is a party we each get started from the minute we start our day. We all get to have our own perspective of life every morning when we wake up. I am grateful I have my very own unique perspective. Imagine life if we all had the same, the very same perspective of life. I might end up having to see the world like the glass half empty folks do, that would be a total nightmare. I'm just say' n....

When we change our perspective we change everything. Perspective is a magic wand, and I don't even have to be holding a stick for it to work. I had a perspective for a long time that if I said or did something the person I was in a relationship with did not like, I was not safe. I had to be perfect to be safe. This perspective generated an amazing sequence of events by me, in a desperate attempt to return to good graces, such that I completely confused and dismayed whoever was around me. It all stopped the day I changed my perspective.

I am grateful I now hold the perspective that I am imperfect and I am safe. Those are the most magical words I have ever thought, or said, or typed on a page. Those words, and that perspective changed my life. I am grateful. I am perfectly imperfectly perfect. I am safe. I am amazed. I am safe. I am imperfect. I am free. I am safe.

Q is for QUIET.

I am not talking about zero-noise quiet here. I can't even imagine zero-noise being possible on our planet. Even if I retreated to nature, on some high mountain top, there would be a bird or a breeze or a burrowing yellow bellied marmot near by. The quiet I am grateful for is the quiet that comes when I can turn off the work noise. By *work* I am referring to job work, house work, kitchen work, laundry work, yard work, day to day living life work, relationship work, all of that work.

The quiet I am grateful for is the quiet my mind finds when I stare into a burning camp fire or watch water roll over rocks in a fast moving stream. It is the quiet that comes when I am in the shower. Who knows why that happens? It is the quiet holding a sleeping newborn baby in my arms brings. It is the quiet that lets me listen beyond words. Quiet comes when I sit in front of my painting wall, paints in the pallet, paint brush in my hand, waiting for the start of the painting to come tell me what to do.

I am grateful for the quiet that shows up when I am immersed in something I love. It is the quiet that comes to me when I am doing something, so deeply from my heart, that time stops and hours fly by. I do not notice it is now dark outside. This is the pay dirt of quiet for me. Everything and everyone falls away and it is just me, and the passion in my heart of hearts, doing a slow dance with purpose and destiny.

R is for RUNNING.

I remember my first pair of "real" running shoes, they were cobalt blue and made by Etonic. I received them as a gift, for which I am still grateful, from Dan Buckstein when we first started dating in 1979. Today I ran in my hot pink Nike "real" running shoes. There have been many pairs of running shoes between that first pair and this pair. I am grateful for them all.

I simply love to run. I love the movement of it. It feels freeing to me. I ran track in grade school. My favorite running is running for me, not for track. My favorite place to run in Denver is Washington Park. It is filled with gardens and other runners, people out there running for the joy of it, just like me. We smile as we pass each other in our understanding of "run joy". I have gone for runs in Olympia, Pueblo, Richland, Hawaii and Mexico. I have run in so many hotel exercise rooms I have lost count. I am grateful for every run, everywhere. I am grateful I can run, that I have a body healthy enough to run.

I just finished running on the Livestrong treadmill Luke and Rebecca gave me for Christmas. I am grateful for my own treadmill. I run any time of the day, and in any weather, in the consistent elements of my basement. Jay gave me a flat screen TV and an Apple TV so I can watch TED Talks while I run. I am grateful to exercise my mind and my body at the same time. There is a connection between my running body and my open mind. I am grateful for the mind-body reminder running provides, because sometimes I forget I have them both!

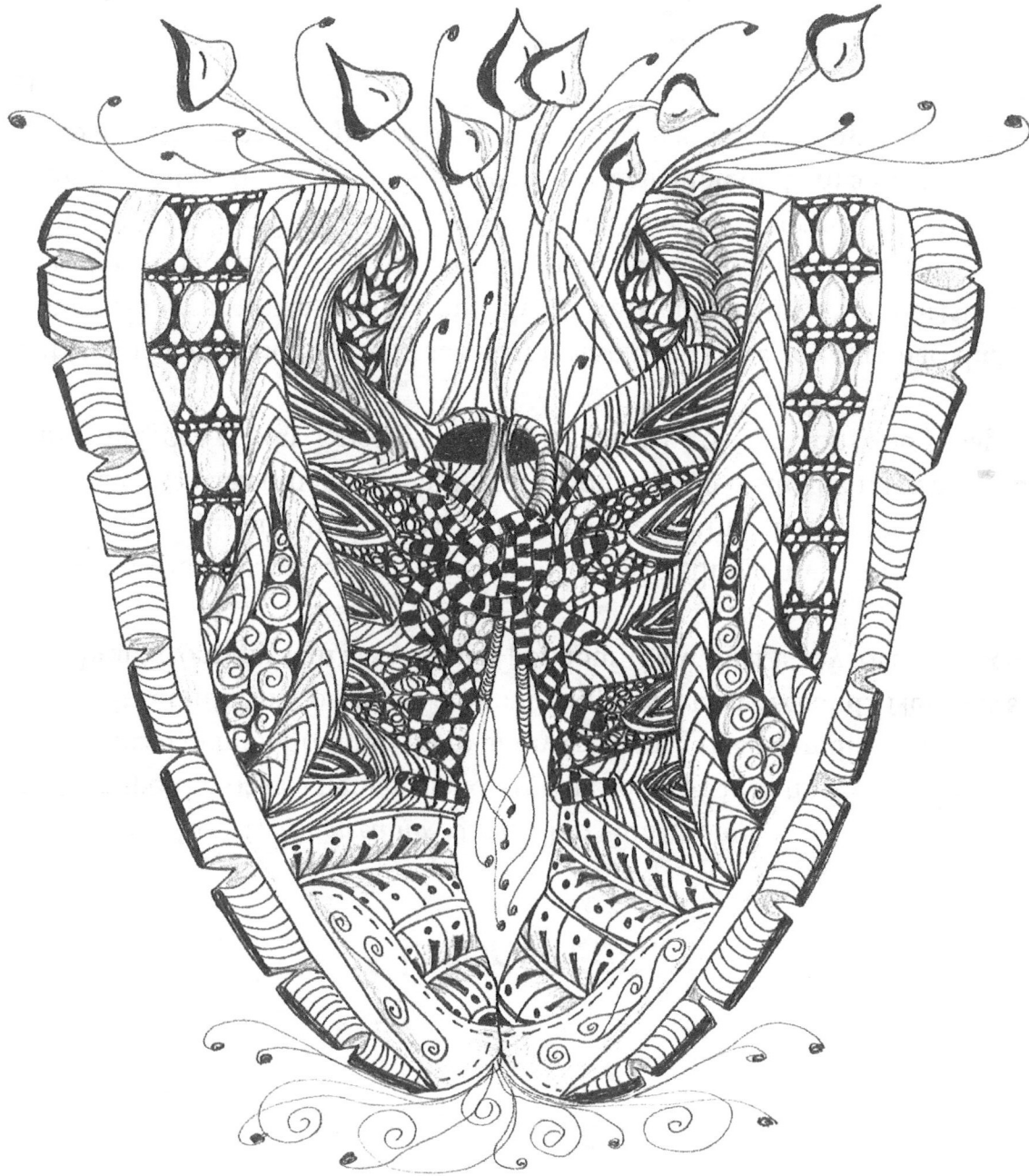

S is for SPEED.

Maverick: *I feel the need...* Goose: *The need for speed.* (Top Gun quote)
I too feel the need for speed, not in a fighter plane. The speed I love is in my brain. That's right,
I am grateful for my speed demon brain up there in my cranium. Twenty-million-million, thats
20,000,000,000,000, bits of information move around in my brain every second. Neurons send
information to my brain from my skin at 150 miles per hour. Now, that is my idea of speed.

I love to explore. It is my nature. I was born this way. Here is the thing: my favorite place to explore is
the universe between my own ears. In this space I can create anything. I love ideas, connecting dots,
taking things not related to each other at all and figuring out how to relate them in some new, all so
creative way. This is my idea of play. Speedy play in the fast plane of my axons and synapses.

There are times it feels like my brain is going so fast it is smoking. Have you ever had that feeling?
There are days I come home from an intense think day at work and say my brain hurts! I love this brain.
I am grateful every morning when I wake up and my speed demon brain kicks in. My brain is ready to
go from the moment I transition from sleep to awake. I can hear its motor running, urging me to put
the pedal to the metal, and let the electric jumping begin! I am grateful I am a morning person. I am
grateful Jay puts up with the morning person I am because I am well aware my vroom vroom brain is
hard to wake up next to.

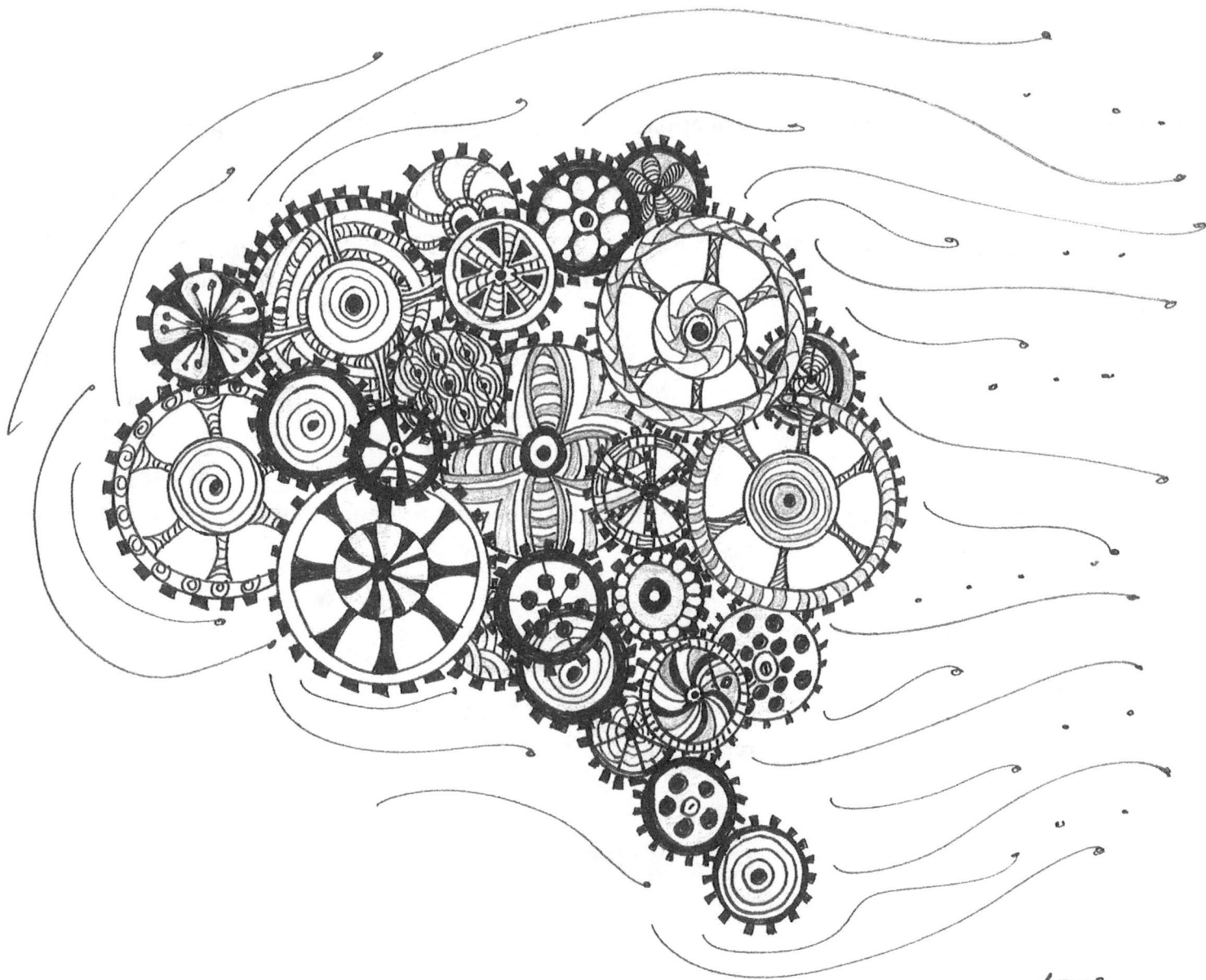

T is for THANK YOU.

I love these two words, thank and you. Put these two words together and you can change someone's day. I know this from when I did a 21 day exercise on happiness. One of the assignments was to do something small and kind for someone everyday. I kept my eyes open for something coworkers did for which I could send a sincere and specific online thank-you note for everyday. I frequently received an email back telling me I had, "Made their day," which, of course, made my day.

Saying thank you means more than those two words imply. It means you noticed, you were looking:
- It means I see you.
- It means you are good.
- It means you did something right.
- It means I liked what you did, which indirectly means I like you. It does.

I sent one of my online thank-you notes to a woman I work with who, to say the least, challenges me. I did it on purpose. I thanked her for her perseverance (she is like a dog with a bone). I don't think it changed her opinion of me. It did change my opinion of her. I decided that was what mattered.

Here is a big hearted energy field, THANK YOU, to everyone who ever touched my life with a kindness.

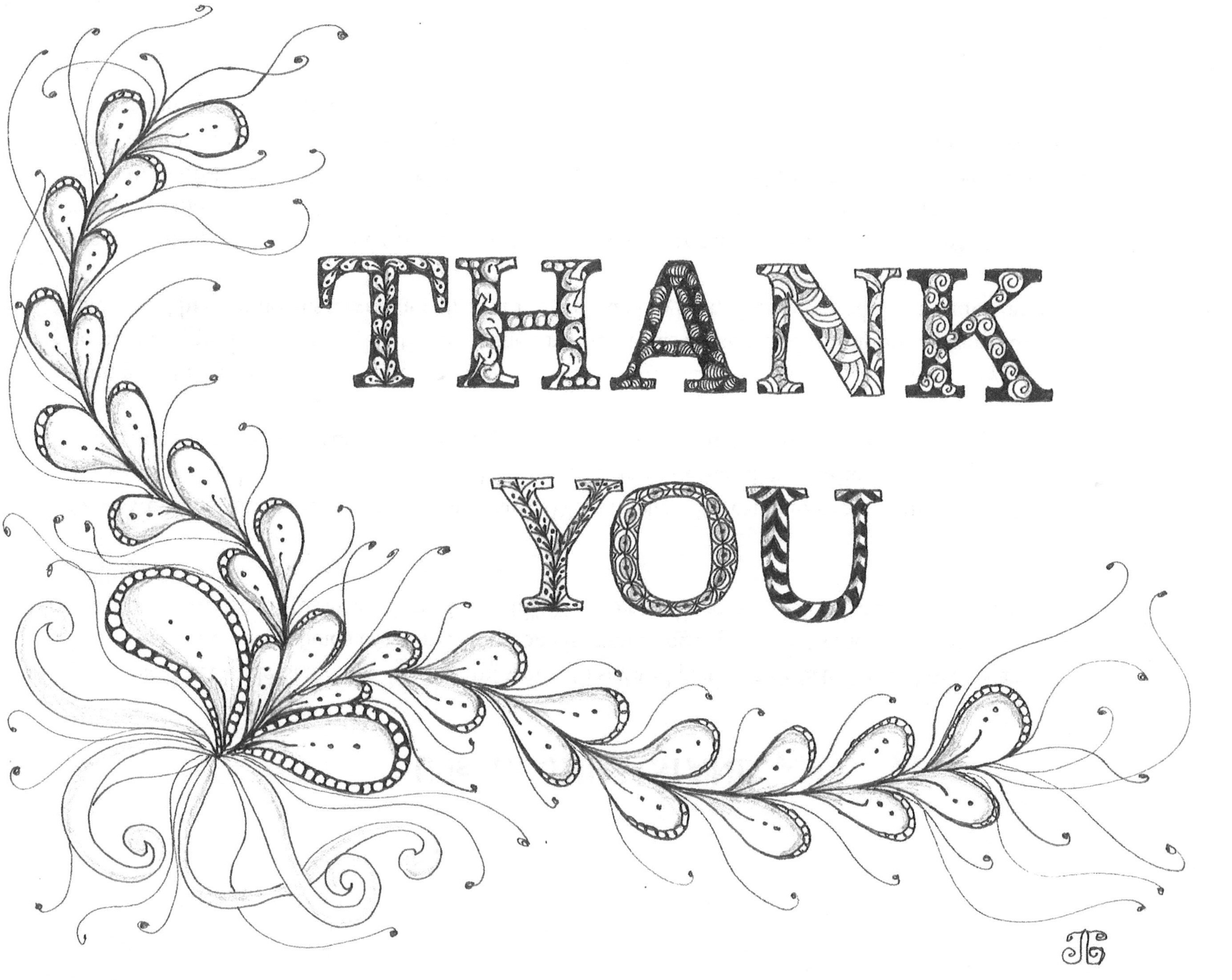
THANK
YOU

U is for UNDERSTAND.

"You just don't understand me" are painful words to say and painful words to hear. We all want to know someone understands us. When someone is expressing anger or extreme disappointment, the most powerful words to say are "I understand". "I understand" means, I hear your words; I hear your feelings; I see you.

Once we feel understood we can take a breath. We can relax. We can allow true conversation to begin. We can stop working to be understood. When countries understand each other peace can form, and it is the same person to person. I can make peace with you if I understand your point of view.

I am grateful every time I can put myself in a place of understanding. I am grateful for every time someone responded with understanding when my heart was broken, and my emotions were running like a wild herd of horses toward a cliff, and I just needed to hear, "I understand, Jo. I understand."

Here is a deep wish, I wish the people in our country could understand each other. I wish there could be true discourse. Discourse that comes from being willing to allow ourselves to be vulnerable enough to understand there are differences, and those differences make us strong, not weak. I wish for compassion deep enough, and strong enough, for people on both sides of any issue to look across the chasm and say, "I understand."

V is for VULNERABILITY.

In her book, *Daring Greatly*, Brené Brown tells me, "Vulnerability is the birthplace of love, belonging, joy, courage, empathy, and creativity." This is a brilliant list. I want these things. Most likely, you want these things too. Are we willing to be truly vulnerable to get them? I am grateful for vulnerability. It changed my life. Being willing to be vulnerable is what changed my perspective (see P is for Perspective) in the magic pixie sort of way. I am grateful for Brené Brown.

I was running on my treadmill, watching Brené Brown's TEDX Houston talk. She is a story teller, a researcher story teller. She had me from the start, but when I heard her say creativity is born of vulnerability, I had to stop running, stand still and listen. Brené defines vulnerability as uncertainty, risk, and emotional exposure. I listened to Brené talk about how we cannot selectively numb emotions. I know creativity eats emotion (energy in motion) for breakfast, lunch and dinner and probably for snacks. It was perfectly clear; I was going to have to be vulnerable if I wanted to regain my lost creative self. In that moment, it was like the door to my authentic self flew open. There was never a door. I made it up.

I am sitting here as I write this thinking about all the actions I took to avoid being vulnerable, all the chaos that caused, and all the reasons why I took those actions. All I can say is, I am grateful. I am vulnerable. I am grateful. The same well dug by my fear of uncertainty, risk, and emotional exposure now holds my vulnerability. From this well I can birth enough creativity for the planet!

W is for WISDOM.

Wikipedia tells me wisdom is defined as: *a deep understanding and realization of people, things, events or situations, resulting in the ability to apply perceptions, judgements and actions in keeping with this understanding*. In all my years of growing up, I have thought of wisdom as something my elders had, and I did not as yet. Now, as I am weeks away from my fifty-eighth birthday, I feel I am the elder. In the Wicca traditions I was taught there are three phases to women: maiden, mother and crone. I am a Crone. Going to Wikipedia again I read, *In some groups croning is a ritual rite of passage into an era of wisdom, freedom, and personal power*. I am a Crone entering an era of wisdom.

The magic in the first definition above, for me, is the part of the sentence that reads, *the ability to apply perceptions, judgements and <u>actions</u> in keeping with this understanding*. I had not thought of wisdom as action until I started this writing tonight. Wisdom is a noun. I thought of it as a way of thinking. I now see this as the source of the personal power mentioned in the second definition above. The power comes when wise thoughts and wise actions travel together. I am grateful I am a Crone in action.

Wisdom comes with a price. In *Abre La Puerta*, Clarissa Pinkola Estes tells us, "*Same old story, all strong souls first go to hell before they do the healing of the world they came here for*. If you live long enough, and have a soul strong enough to go to hell and come back, you can gain the wisdom and take the actions to do the healing you came here to do. I am grateful for healing actions. I am grateful I am a creativity healing Crone.

X is for X CHROMOSOME.

There it is, the reason I am a woman. I have two X Chromosomes. XX for a girl. XY for a boy. I was a Tomboy growing up. I could play cars and trucks in the dirt with my brother Paul for hours and days and no one blinked an eye. Paul could not play dolls with me, there would have been more than blinking eyes. Our dad would have stopped him. I have always been grateful to be a woman. As a girl it seemed to me I had more choices. Imagine my surprise when I learned *little girls do, grown women do not*, in some countries even today that is true in mind blowing ways.

There are still glass ceilings here in the USA as Hillary Clinton pointed during her first run for President. I prefer to look at the glass half full though and celebrate my little girl view. I still believe I get more choices:

- I can wear any clothes I want to--pants, dresses, skirts. The only men in skirts are the ones in kilts.
- I get to accessorize with jewelry, wild hair, crazy socks, big boots, fake fur coats and no one will blink. Men can do those things--but people will blink.
- I can be as strong or a weak as I want, my choice. No one expects me to stay on my white horse.
- I can show ALL of my emotions. Enough said.
- I have never been turned down for a job I wanted because I am a woman. Luckily I live now, not every day before and up through the 1950's.

Women have the ultimate "can do." We give birth. For now, that is also a choice. I am grateful.

Y is for YEARNING.

I long to yearn. To have something I want so deeply I can say I yearn for it. I want this because it means I will be filled with passion and desire. Life should be lived for the people and the actions we yearn for. Perhaps this yearning rides along with wisdom. The yearning to put action with wisdom. It felt that way when I wrote *W is for Wisdom*. As I wrote, I yearned to take action in keeping with my wise crone understandings.

A few years ago I yearned to have someone kind in my life, truly kind and caring. Someone who would help me build up what I wanted to grow bigger, not teach me hard lessons about what to let go of. I'd had enough of the hard relationship lessons in life. Deep yearning must have magic built into it. I have Jay. Jay is kind. Jay is caring. Jay helps me build. He helps me get where I want to go and I am not just talking about Paris.

Now I yearn to help others. I yearn to help others find their creative confidence they lost along the way when someone told them they could not draw or dance or sing or that their sculpture did not look like a horse as David Kelley tells in his inspiring TED talk. I yearn to create a creative confidence curriculum which can reach from junior high to graduate level. I yearn to somehow touch off the creative spark in everyone I meet. I yearn to teach that creativity creates creativity.

Z is for ZOE.

A little sprite named Zoe arrived in our lives on October 17, 2011. Jay and I are thrilled to be Zoe's Great Uncle and Great Aunt. I am grateful to Jessa and Grant for having Zoe. I am grateful to Zoe for teaching me to see the world through "new arrival" eyes again. Zoe has an endless lists of firsts. They all fascinate her. Life fascinates her. She watches. She listens. She touches. She reacts. She reacts authentically. She learns. She grows. She changes. She does it all over again.

Zoe is still pure creativity. She creates games. She holds a piece of cheese out for Jay and then snatches it away. She giggles in delight of her created play. She plays hide and seek, in public. She never thinks about who is looking at her or what they will think. She knows what she wants and what she does not want. In a big way, she knows when she wants it and when she does not want it.

When Zoe sees someone she likes, her face lights up with delight, and her hands wiggle with excitement. She shows it all. She holds nothing back. The person she is reacting to feels like a ray of sunshine touched them in her smile! They light up in return. When was the last time I showed all my delight at seeing you? When did I get to see you light up in return? I am grateful to Zoe for the reminder. Letting some of my delight out--only some of it is such a sad waste. I want to be more like Zoe, who at one year old, was filled with the wonder of life new.

www.ingramcontent.com/pod-product-compliance
Lightning Source LLC
Chambersburg PA
CBHW081724270326
41933CB00017B/3288